ALL-STAR WRESTLING

HULK HOGAN

PHOTOGRAPHIC CREDITS

BRUCE BENNETT: COVER, 19, 25, 29
FOCUS WEST, WILLIAM HART: 6
SYGMA, TOM BUCHANAN: 15
SYGMA, STEVE TAYLOR: 9
WIDE WORLD PHOTOS: 2 & 3, 13, 23

Published by Creative Education, Inc., 123 South Broad Street, Mankato, Minnesota 56001

Library of Congress Catalog Card No.: 86-72533

ISBN 0-88682-087-1

ALL-STAR WRESTLING

HULK HOGAN

BY DON WARD

CREATIVE EDUCATION

Trivia Question ... Okay, you probably know that Hulk is 6-foot-7 and weighs in at a trim 300 pounds in his wrestling shorts. Maybe you even know that he was born in Tampa, Florida where he first wrestled under the ring names Terry Boulder and Sterling Golden.

Now award yourself the International Hulk Trivia Cup if you can blurt out Hulk's real name. Give up? Hulk's mom named her chubby little son Terry Jean Bolette.

☆ ☆ ☆

Playing In Pain ... Then there was the famous 1986 Madison Square Garden show when 22,000 fans showed up to watch Hulk Hogan go against Randy "Macho Man" Savage. The trouble was, Hulk had suffered a concussion, several muscle tears and rib damage in an earlier bout that week against King Kong Bundy.

Lesser athletes might have backed out of the

Garden bout, but Hogan gulped a couple aspirin, taped up his ribs and went on with the show. Poor Randy Savage.

☆ ☆ ☆

Quick Worker ... Hulk won the AWA World Championship on January 23, 1984 by stopping his royal nastiness The Iron Sheik in a mere five minutes. Since then, the Hulkster has taken on a steady stream of challengers, winning each and every bout in 10 minutes or less!

☆ ☆ ☆

Play It Again, Hulk ... Hogan had his eye on becoming a rock 'n' roll star long before promoters Jack and Jerry Brisco coaxed him into the ring.

"I can play guitar real pretty," grunts Hulk whenever he's asked about the years he plucked

for a living in smoky little nightclubs.

"He can play the piano, too," claims wacky rock star and wrestling enthusiast Cyndi Lauper. "He holds it in one hand and plays with the other."

☆ ☆ ☆

Hulk's Hair Saved By Hillbilly Jim ... It looked bad for the Hulk one night in Bradford, Ontario. Big John Studd and Ken Patera had ganged up on Hogan in an effort to take the scissors to his famous golden hair. Just as they were about to do the crewcut routine, however, a fan leaped suddenly through the ropes to save the day for the Hulk.

That "fan" turned out to be Jim Morris, a young, third-rate grappler from Kentucky whose dream was to crack the wrestling big-time. Hulk, who figured he owed Jim a favor for helping him escape from a scalping, decided to take the kid under his wing.

After training with the world champ for almost a year, "Hillbilly" Jim Morris is now realizing his dream. Today, he is one of the WWF's most popular stars. Now Hulk finds himself in the strange position of facing the man he trained—the only wrestler in the world who knows all Hogan's secrets!

☆ ☆ ☆

Hulk Trademarks . . . The Hulk has style, that's for certain.

His theme song: The sudden tribal sound of "Eye Of The Tiger" alerts the audience that the champ is about to leave his dressing room.

His grand entry: With massive arms swinging crazily, Hulk strides like a man possessed toward the ring. Already, his white-gold hair and Fu-Manchu moustache are drenched with sweat.

His psyche job: Once inside the ropes, he thrusts his finger above his head, rolls his flashing eyes, tears off his Hulk-a-mania T-Shirt and tosses the pieces to the frenzied crowd.

His performance: Swift and sure. No man lasts longer than a few short minutes with the champ.

☆ ☆ ☆

Muhammad Hogan ... It is often said that the extraordinary talent and flair of Muhammad Ali breathed new life into professional boxing just in the nick of time. What Ali did to revive boxing, Hulk Hogan has done for professional wrestling.

"Overnight, thanks to Hulk Hogan, pro wrestling has jumped from little smoke-filled arenas to multi-million-dollar bouts on HBO," says promoter George Hart. "Without Hulk, we would've never seen the likes of WrestleMania."

In case you missed them, WrestleMania I and II were the first professional wrestling events to combine top Hollywood stars with world-class wrestlers in a nationally-televised entertainment special.

At WrestleMania, Mr. T teamed up with Hulk Hogan. (The next week, Hulk became the first wrestler in history to make the cover of Sports Illustrated).

Joan Rivers, William Perry, Susan St. James, Ray Charles, Cyndi Lauper and other celebrities entertained the fans between bouts. And both WrestleMania cards were televised to millions of homes and closed-circuit viewers throughout the country. In fact, more people saw WrestleMania II than have seen any wrestling card in the history of the sport.

☆ ☆ ☆

Teaming Up With Mr. T ... It was the devil's own dream match, and it happened in front of more than one million viewers as the featured bout in WrestleMania.

Hulk Hogan and the infamous Mr. T of A-Team fame were in one corner. Over in the other cor-

ner paced Paul Orndorff and Rowdy Roddy Piper.

Those who may have wondered whether Mr. T was for real got a glimpse that night of an outstanding athlete with the courage of 10 men. Though Piper (voted the most-hated man in wrestling in the People's poll for three years straight) pulled every vile, nasty trick in the book, somehow Mr. T held on.

"It's too bad you can't open up a man's chest to get a look at his heart," said Hulk in admiration as he savored the victory. "If you could, you'd see a mighty big one in my partner, Mr. T!"

☆ ☆ ☆

King Kong ... When Hogan agreed to meet King Kong Bundy in a steel cage match in WrestleMania II, Hulk fans held their breath.

At 6-foot-5 and 480 pounds, Bundy moves around the ring with the speed of a man half his size. His background as an All-American wrestler in high school and college propelled him into the pros, where he was taught scientific wrestling by the great Von Erich family. Now add the fact that Bundy has a history of going temporarily insane inside the ring, and you can share the concern of Hulk's growing legion of loyal fans.

In WrestleMania II, however, Hulk used the match-up with Bundy to showcase his full range of talents, once and for all. Despite several close calls in which Bundy nearly crunched Hulk with his hated avalanche move, Hogan eventually climbed out of the cage first, leaving behind a badly beaten Bundy.

"I had a secret reason for wanting to humiliate Bundy," growled Hulk after the match. "People been saying that I don't have any moves—that I can't keep up with the fancy scientific guys. Well, the whole world saw me do the job on Bundy and now you know. Science don't stand a chance against Hulk man!"

Tough luck, Bundy. You had your shot against the real king—and blew it!

☆ ☆ ☆

But, Can He Wrestle? ... Virtually everyone agrees that Hulk Hogan has done more than any other champion in history to promote the popularity of wrestling. Indeed, it has been estimated that attendance at wrestling events around the country has nearly tripled since Hogan captured the championship belt.

Oddly enough, however, the Hulk is continuously criticized by large numbers of die-hard wrestling fans who maintain that he lacks the wrestling skills of a true champion.

"Let's face it," says veteran matchmaker Larry Carlson, "Hulk is a fantastic athlete, but his technique is still very rough in certain ways. His strength, intelligence and speed have pulled him

out of many bad situations that a better wrestler would have never gotten into in the first place.

"Of course, you can criticize the man all day long, but the bottom line is that he always finds a way to win. That, in my mind, is the mark of a true champ."

☆ ☆ ☆

Hardy-Har-Har, Hulk ... Detractors of Hulk Hogan—and there are a few—like to read Charles Russo's columns and articles. Russo is one of those guys who speaks his mind, and he has a way of saying a whole lot in just a few words. While most wrestling writers these days are going on and on about the seemingly endless string of outrageous exploits in the continuing Hulkamania saga, Russo came right to the point in the Feedback section of Wrestling 86:

"Hulk Hogan. Flex. Grimace. Shout. Brawl. Wrestle? Har-hardy-har-har. Play with dolls. Play with thumb-wrestlers. Watch cartoons. Commercialize in general. Flex more. Grimace more. Shout more. No more! World champ? Ho-hum."

☆ ☆ ☆

Lumberjack Match ... Randy "Macho Man" Savage is the only man to ever defeat Hogan more than once. The problem is, Savage has resorted to trickery to do it.

Macho Man's favorite tactic is to leap outside the ring whenever he's the least bit winded or in trouble. Naturally, Hulk goes right after him, but Savage has an ace up his trunks. As Hulk chases him around the arena, Savage keeps close track of the referee's count, knowing full well that Hulk will be too frustrated or angry to do the same.

Then, at the count of 9, Savage will suddenly leap into the ring, leaving Hulk stranded at the final count of 10. Result: Hulk defeated by a count out—a cheap victory, but a victory nonetheless for Macho Man.

Finally, however, Hulk has come up with a sure-fire solution called a "Lumberjack Match." In this unique wrestling format, the entire ring is surrounded by other wrestlers. If either Hogan or Savage tries to leave the ring, they will be thrown back in by their peers. Trapped like a rat. Now what, Randy?

☆ ☆ ☆

Rocky III ... Despite his current All-American image, let's not forget that Hogan started out in the sport as a nasty, rule-breaking bad guy. He was booed from coast-to-coast for several years before a big break changed his image and his life.

That break came when Hollywood actor Sly Stallone saw The Hulkster on TV one day and instantly decided that he was the man he wanted to play the rotten-egg wrestler in Rocky II. The rest is history. The movie went gangbusters and Hogan found himself riding a groundswell of growing

national fame. Wham! No more Mr. Bad Guy. Overnight, The Hulk became a peachy guy.

☆ ☆ ☆

Through Japanese Eyes ... On a recent tour through the Orient, The Hulk was soundly thrashed in front of 13,000 fans by Antonio Inoki, the National Wrestling hero of Japan. Hulk retained his title, however, because Inoki won by count-out when Hulk was unable to return to the ring in time. (A champ can only lose his title through pin or submission).

In an exclusive article for Main Event, Japanese wrestling analyst Kazu Masanabe gave this account of the honorable Hulk:

"Although Hulk Hogan demonstrated a noble and even exemplary pride in upholding American values, many fans here were disappointed that he chose to brawl instead of display classic wrestling skills.

"Our conclusion is that it is very easy to be deceived by Hulk Hogan. Certainly he is a fine athlete and a charismatic personality. Too often, however, he relies on his size to win. We cannot consider this honorable. In Japan, we value wrestling, not fighting, and there are unwritten rules to which an honorable wrestler must adhere. We do not dismiss brawling as a valid technique, but there must be more.

"Also, American promoters do not provide Hogan with adequate competition. We understand your system, and the popularity of the WWF champion, but one does not meditate for money. It is not honorable."

☆ ☆ ☆

The Latest Scouting Report ... Wrestling Superstars Magazine recently concluded an in-depth analysis of the Top 20 Wrestlers in the nation. Get this: After all was said and done, Hulk—the world champ—finished in a tie for 9th place!

What gives? Well, the ranking was based on a system in which each individual is ranked against his peers, regardless of weight. Each wrestler was rated in 10 categories on a scale of 1 to 10, with 10 being the top score.

Hulk's low score even surprised the editors of the magazine, but here is the way they put the full bad news/good news report:

Hulk lacks scientific knowledge and takes a tremendous amount of punishment for a man his size ... Relies greatly on his size and power ... At 6-foot-8, 302 pounds, Hogan is an awesome sight in the ring and very hard to outbrawl ... Has the ability to simply overwhelm an opponent.

One of only three rated wrestlers to earn a 10.0 in as many as three categories (conditioning, power, and ability to absorb punishment) ... A superb physical specimen, Hogan has undertaken an intense gym regimen and figures to get even stronger.

Speculation about ligament damage to Hogan's knee persists ... Able to bounce back from adversity ... Is helped by the WWF's policy against matching fan favorites.

His limited offense can hurt him severely in a match against somebody with scientific knowledge. This is a serious blemish on his championship record.

☆ ☆ ☆

Hulk-A-Money ... Believe it or not, The Hulk is thought to be the highest-paid athlete in the world of sport. He is the IBM of wrestling—a living, breathing, brawling, golden-haired Fort Knox.

Figure it out. Beyond millions of dollars per year in direct ring earnings, Hulk makes countless public appearances at thousands of dollars apiece.

There are Hulk videos. Hulk T-shirts, dolls, toothbrushes, drinking cups, lunch buckets, games and novelties. A Hulk cartoon show. Televison roles on

The Love Boat, Search For Tomorrow, The A-Team, etc. Celebrity events with various rock stars, including Cyndi Lauper, Bruce Springsteen and others.

"Based on my estimates," says wrestling expert Jerry Forbes, "if The Hulk were working a normal 40-hour week for 50 weeks a year, he'd be earning the equivalent of $2,500 per hour, or $20,000 per day, or $100,000 per week!"

☆ ☆ ☆

Poetry In Motion ... The Hulk gets enough fan mail these days to start his own post office, but we like the following little ditty submitted for Hulk via Wrestling World Mag by Phylis Kerns of Baltimore, Maryland:

The Hulkster
Hulk Hogan is still number one,
He's the champ, the big gun!
Most opponents look like clowns,

Trying to put the mighty champ down.
Some try to pin him to the mat.
But they wind up flat on their backs!
He's the greatest champion of all,
He answers every challenger's call.
He's an awesome figure in the ring
And Hulkamaniacs surround the ring!
Muscles ripple beneath his golden tan
The arena's packed with Hulkster fans!
He's a warm man with a heart of gold.
Most deserving of the gold he holds!
Hulk Hogan is the champion's name,
Wrestling is his claim to fame.
I hope Hulk remains champ for years,
For the world has only begun to cheer!
Hulk, you're honest, brave, and true,
The U.S. is proud to have a champ like you!